Reindeer

A Fun and Educational Book for Kids with Amazing Facts and Pictures

Table of Contents

Introduction

The northern hemisphere's tundra, boreal woods, and hilly regions are home to the reindeer, sometimes known as caribou, a species of deer. They have various distinctive morphological and behavioral traits that enable them to survive in extreme temperatures, and they are well adapted to surviving in cold habitats.

The unique antlers of reindeer, which are typically only found on males, are well known (although some females also have them). They compete for mate rights and hunt for food, among other things, with their antlers. Wide hooves are another characteristic of reindeer, which enable them to go across soft ground and deep snow.

Since ancient times, mankind have tamed reindeer, particularly the indigenous populations of the Arctic. They are employed as a cultural emblem, as well as for transportation, their meat, milk, and hides. Reindeer are crucial to many indigenous societies' ceremonial and religious practices. Also, due to their link with Santa Claus in popular culture, reindeer are frequently connected with Christmas.

Scientific Name

Rangifer tarandus is the name given to reindeer by scientists.

Appearance

Reindeer can survive in cold and severe situations thanks to a number of unique physical traits. Deer of this species are usually of middle size, with males being larger than females. Their main physical characteristics include:

Both male and female reindeer have antlers, although the males' often grow larger and more prominent antlers. Antlers are shed and regrown every year, and they are used for fighting and display during mating season.

Fur: The thick, two-layered coat of fur on reindeer is made up of an undercoat that acts as insulation and a topcoat that is longer and coarser. They are protected from wind and snow by their fur, which also keeps them warm in cold weather.

Wide, cloven hooves on reindeer allow them to move easily across ice and snow. The animal's weight is dispersed across a wider area by the hooves, which act as snowshoes to keep the animal from sinking into the snow.

Color: The brownish-gray coat of reindeer varies significantly in hue depending on the season. Its fur is typically darker in the winter to help them blend in with the snow, and lighter in the summer.

Size: A reindeer's length is typically between 1.2 and 2.2 meters (4–7 feet) and its shoulder height is roughly 1.2 meters (4 ft). In general, male reindeer are bigger than female reindeer, and certain subspecies are bigger than others.

Geography

The Arctic tundra, boreal forests, and mountainous regions of the world are where reindeer are most commonly found. There are reindeer in a number of nations, such as:

Norway: The northern regions of Norway, particularly the county of Finnmark, are home to reindeer.

Sweden: Reindeer are located in the country's northern regions, and herding them is a significant aspect of Sami culture there.

Finland: Lapland, in particular, is home to many reindeer.

Russia: Siberia and the Arctic are two of the country's northernmost places where reindeer can be found.

Canada: The Arctic territories of Nunavut, the Northwest Territories, and Yukon are home to a number of reindeer.

Alaska: Reindeer may be found all over the state, and herding has played a significant role in its history and culture.

Moreover, reindeer have been brought to Iceland, Greenland, and other regions of northern Europe.

Behavior

Although smaller groups are more typical, reindeer live in herds of up to several hundred individuals. Their main behavioral traits include, among others:

Migration: Every year, a large number of populations of reindeer travel long distances in search of food and to avoid the harsh winter weather. Depending on the region and subspecies of reindeer, these migrations vary in duration and timing.

Diet: Reindeer consume a range of plants, including lichens, mosses, grasses, and shrubs. They are herbivores. When food is scarce in the winter, they may search through snow for food or nibble on bark and twigs.

Reindeer communicate with one another by using a variety of vocalizations, body language cues, and scent marking. For instance, during mating season, males may utilize a vocalization called a "click" to establish dominance.

A thick coat of fur, unique hooves that help them move

through snow, and a slow metabolic rate that enables them to preserve energy are just a few of the adaptations reindeer have that help them survive in cold climates.

Reindeer herds feature a hierarchy within which powerful animals are given access to the finest food and breeding possibilities. A common method of establishing dominance is through combat sports like antler wrestling.

Indigenous populations in the Arctic areas have been domesticating reindeer for thousands of years. Domesticated reindeer are an integral part of many indigenous people' cultures and are utilized for transportation, milk, meat, and hides.

Reproduction

Depending on the population, the mating season for reindeer can range anywhere from a few weeks to many months. Reindeer normally mate in the fall or early winter. The following are some essential elements of reindeer reproduction:

Male reindeer will compete for access to females during the mating season. Physical competitions, such as antler wrestling, are frequently involved in this, with dominant males having the best chances of mating.

Birth and gestation: Female reindeer normally give birth to a single calf in late spring or early summer after a gestation period of about 7-8 months. Soon after birth, calves can stand and run, and by the following winter, they are typically weaned.

Parental care: Female reindeer tend to their young in the majority, while males may also assist in defending and protecting the herd. It is crucial for adults to provide protection for calves since they are weak against predators like wolves and bears.

Longevity and reproduction: Although reindeer can survive up to 15 years in the wild, many do not because of sickness, predators, and other problems. Male reindeer may not attain sexual maturity until they are 5–6 years old, whereas female reindeer normally start reproducing at around 2-3 years of age.

Social Life

Reindeer are herd-living, gregarious creatures that can number anywhere from a few to several hundred. Their main social tendencies include:

Reindeer live in herds to protect themselves because it is simpler to notice predators and defend against attacks when they are grouped together. In order to locate food and water, herds may work together.

Social hierarchy exists in reindeer herds, with the dominant individuals having access to the best food and breeding possibilities. A common method of establishing dominance is through combat sports like antler wrestling.

Reindeer communicate with one another by using a variety of vocalizations, body language cues, and scent marking. For instance, during mating season, males may utilize a vocalization called a "click" to establish dominance.

Group defense: To protect themselves against predators,

reindeer may employ a number of tactics, such as clustering together, circling the attacker, or even attacking with their antlers.

Herding behavior: Reindeer may move as a group to avoid danger or to reach a new site when migrating or when they are being hunted.

Domestication: Over thousands of years, indigenous people in the Arctic areas have tamed reindeer, which now play a significant part in their culture and social structures. A single herder or an entire community may take care of the herds of domesticated reindeer.

Habitat

Across the Northern Hemisphere, reindeer can be found in a range of environments, including mountainous areas, subarctic woodlands, and Arctic tundra. They can live in places with a lot of snow, chilly temperatures, and sparse vegetation since they are well adapted to life in cold climates.

Permafrost, a layer of continuously frozen earth, dominates the terrain of the Arctic tundra, where reindeer are most frequently found, preventing the establishment of trees and other flora. Reindeer eat lichens, mosses, grasses, and other vegetation that can thrive in the hard conditions in order to survive in this environment.

Reindeer may consume a range of tree species as well as grasses and other ground plants in subarctic woods. They may live in high-altitude meadows and slopes in hilly areas, grazing on alpine plants.

In addition to being able to adjust to seasonal habitat changes, reindeer are also capable of making long migrations in search of food and to avoid inclement weather. While some populations may move between lowland and highland habitats, others may migrate between summer and winter ranges.

Senses

Due to their highly acute senses, reindeer are able to navigate their surroundings and escape predators. Their main senses include the following:

Reindeer can sense movement and distinguish between different hues thanks to their keen vision. This aids them in spotting predators and navigating their surroundings.

Smell: Reindeer have a keen sense of smell and can identify other reindeer, potential food sources, and predators from a great distance. Via scent marking, reindeer may communicate with one another using their sense of smell.

Hearing: Reindeer have keen hearing and can distinguish a variety of sounds. This enables them to recognize predators and vocally interact with one another.

Touch: Due to their sensitive skin, reindeer are able to feel changes in wind, temperature, and other environmental conditions. By doing so, they are better able to control their body temperature and move around their surroundings.

In general, these senses aid reindeer in navigating their surroundings, avoiding predators, and interacting with one another. Because of these crucial adaptations, reindeer have been able to live and thrive in their native Arctic and sub-Arctic settings.

Feeding

Being herbivores, reindeer eat primarily vegetation, such as grasses, sedges, mosses, lichens, and bushes. Their feeding habits have been modified to fit their nutrient-poor, sparsely vegetated Arctic and sub-Arctic settings. One of the most important elements of reindeer eating behavior is:

Reindeer forage on grasses and shrubs, making them both grazers and browsers. They may graze on grasses and other vegetation in the tundra during the summer, and they may browse on shrubs and lichens during the winter.

Reindeer have various adaptations that enable them to absorb nutrients from low-quality food, such as their capacity to digest cellulose and their intricate digestive system. These adaptations help reindeer survive on diets lacking in nutrition. Also, they might only eat specific plant types that are rich in nutrients.

Dietary changes with the seasons: Depending on the time of year and the food supply, reindeer may alter their dietary habits. In order to conserve energy throughout the winter, when food may be in short supply, they may rely more heavily on their fat reserves.

Reindeer may forage in groups, which can serve to keep them safe from predators and improve their foraging productivity. During migration, they might group together into herds, which can aid in locating fresh food sources.

Overall, reindeer have a highly evolved feeding behavior that enables them to obtain nutrition from their surroundings, especially in the harsh Arctic and sub-Arctic climates.

Diet

Being herbivores, plants make up a large portion of the diet of reindeer. They have evolved to thrive in severe Arctic and sub-Arctic regions where vegetation can be sparse, therefore their diet varies depending on the season and the availability of food. Some essential elements of their diet are:

Lichens: In the tundra regions, where other food sources may be rare, lichens represent a significant part of the reindeer's winter diet. Due to a unique digestive system, reindeer can digest lichens' cellulose and extract nutrients from them.

Grasses and sedges: In the tundra and sub-Arctic regions during the summer, when flora is more abundant, reindeer may eat grasses and sedges as food. These plants offer crucial elements including protein and carbs.

Shrubs and woody plants: During the winter, when there are few alternative food sources available, reindeer may also eat shrubs and woody plants. They could graze on the twigs and leaves of birch, willow, and other woody plants.

In some areas, reindeer may also consume mosses and ferns as food sources since they contain vital vitamins and minerals.

Overall, the diversified diet of reindeer enables them to absorb nutrients from a variety of different plant species. They have many modifications that enable them to obtain nutrients from low-quality foliage, and their feeding behavior has been modified to fit the harsh settings they live in.

Babies

Calves, the name for newborn reindeer, are normally born in the late spring or early summer. Important details regarding young reindeer include:

Size and weight: At birth, reindeer calves are rather large, weighing between 5 and 20 kg (11 to 44 lb). To keep them warm in the winter, they are born with a thick covering of fur.

Mobility: After a few hours of birth, reindeer calves can run and walk. By doing so, they may stay with the herd and fend off predators.

Feeding: For the first several months of their lives, reindeer calves are solely dependent on their mother's milk. During a few weeks of birth, they may begin to nibble on foliage, but they do not begin to eat solid food until they are a few months old.

Protection: Mother reindeer are fiercely protective of their young, protecting them from wolves and bears. The herd may surround the calves in a circle to protect them as well.

Growth and development: Within the first month of life, reindeer calves may gain as much as twice their original weight. Before becoming entirely independent, they could spend up to a year living with their mother.

Generally, young reindeer are well suited to live in the severe Arctic and sub-Arctic conditions. They can move swiftly, consume mother's milk, and are shielded by both their mother and the herd.

Predators

There are a number of natural predators of reindeer, including:

One of the principal predators of reindeer is the wolf. In the winter, when other prey is limited, they may hunt individual reindeer or focus on herds.

Brown bears: During the summer when they are foraging for food in the open tundra, brown bears are more likely to prey on reindeer. Because they are more vulnerable than adults, brown bears may also hunt calves.

Arctic foxes: Arctic foxes eat carrion left by other predators as well as reindeer calves.

Golden eagles: During the winter, when reindeer are more susceptible, golden eagles may attack on young or weak reindeer.

The speed and agility of reindeer, their capacity to create protective herds, and their highly developed senses are just a few of the adaptations they have made to help them evade predators. For instance, the excellent senses of smell and hearing that reindeer possess enable them to see predators at a distance. In order to find food or avoid predators, they may even dig through the snow with their hooves.

Evolution

The family Cervidae, which also contains deer, elk, and moose, includes reindeer, which are often referred to as caribou in North America. This family's evolution began in the early Eocene period, some 50 million years ago. The reindeer is one of many kinds of deer and related creatures that have developed over time.

Around 2.5 million years ago, during the Pleistocene era, the first reindeer appeared in the Arctic region. This early reindeer resembled current reindeer in size and appearance, but they had shorter legs and a stronger head. They had to survive the harsh Arctic environment, where the winters were lengthy and bitterly cold, and there were few food supplies available.

In the north of Europe, Asia, and North America, reindeer populations grew as a result of climate change and glacier retreat. Several reindeer subspecies have evolved over time to adapt to the particular environmental circumstances of their area. For male-on-male rivalry, some groups evolved larger antlers, while others evolved more effective digestive systems to draw nutrients from poor-quality food.

In general, reindeer's adaptations to the harsh Arctic climate and interactions with other species, such as predators and people, have affected their evolution. Reindeer are still a significant component of Arctic ecosystems and a valuable resource for many Indigenous peoples today.

Population

Due to regional and subspecies differences, it is challenging to determine the global reindeer population. There are, however, a few hundred thousand cultivated reindeer and an estimated 2.5 million wild reindeer in the world.

Arctic and subarctic regions of North America, Europe, and Asia are home to reindeer populations. Alaska, Canada, and Greenland are home to the largest numbers of caribou (a subspecies of reindeer) in North America, while the northern United States has lesser populations. Scandinavia, Russia, Mongolia, and some regions of China are home to reindeer in both Europe and Asia.

Many variables, including habitat loss, climate change, predation, and hunting, have had an effect on reindeer populations. Due to overhunting or competition from domestic reindeer, reindeer populations have decreased in several locations. Yet, thanks to conservation efforts and hunting limitations in other places, reindeer numbers have grown.

Generally, reindeer populations are appreciated for their cultural, ecological, and economic significance and constitute a significant component of many Arctic and subarctic ecosystems.

Conservation Status

Depending on the subspecies and the area, the conservation status of reindeer varies, although several populations are currently under threat and are thought to be of conservation concern.

According to the International Union for Conservation of Nature (IUCN), numerous reindeer subspecies are either fragile or on the verge of extinction. The Svalbard reindeer (Rangifer tarandus platyrhynchus) is found in Norway, the Taimyr reindeer (Rangifer tarandus sibiricus) is found in Russia, and the woodland caribou (Rangifer tarandus caribou) is found in Canada.

Overhunting and poaching, habitat loss and fragmentation brought on by development and climate change, predation by wolves and other predators, and diseases introduced by tamed reindeer are the greatest threats to reindeer populations.

Reindeer populations are being preserved through the creation of protected areas, habitat restoration, limitations on hunting and poaching, and analysis of the effects of climate change and other dangers. Also, attempts to conserve reindeer maintain the traditional ways of life of numerous Indigenous peoples and local communities, who depend on them for their subsistence and cultural practices.

All things considered, reindeer conservation is a difficult and continuing task that needs the support and involvement of a wide range of stakeholders, including scientists, decision-makers, and local populations.

Health

In general, reindeer are strong creatures who have adapted successfully to the harsh Arctic climate. Nonetheless, they can be prone to a variety of illnesses and health problems, just like all other animals.

The transmission of infections by domesticated reindeer is one of the biggest risks to reindeer's health. Many diseases, including brucellosis, which can have major health effects in wild reindeer populations, can be spread by domesticated reindeer.

Moreover, parasites like lungworms and liver flukes, which can disrupt the digestive and respiratory systems of reindeer, can infect them. Moreover, they may suffer from nutritional inadequacies, especially in the wintertime when food supplies are few.

The alteration of their habitat and food sources brought on by climate change is having an impact on reindeer as well. In addition to increased predation and competition with other species, this may result in hunger, illness, and other problems.

Reindeer populations are kept in good health by keeping an eye out for illnesses, giving them extra food during the winter, and preserving their habitat and food sources. The management of grazing grounds and the use of medicinal herbs to treat illnesses are only two examples of the traditional knowledge and methods that many Indigenous peoples and local communities have that support the preservation of reindeer herds.

Lifespan

Reindeer longevity varies according on things like subspecies, sex, and environmental conditions. Due to things like predators, harsh environments, and food competition, wild reindeer typically live shorter lives than tamed reindeer.

Male reindeer often live to be 10 to 12 years old, whereas female reindeer typically live to be 15 to 18 years old. Some people can live far longer than others, with some wild reindeer living to be over 20 years old.

Some domesticated reindeer can live to be beyond 25 years old and have extended lifespans. They receive better feed, veterinary care, and safety from predators and other dangers as a result.

Overall, a variety of factors, including genetics, nutrition, the environment, the presence of predators and disease, and environmental conditions, affect the lifetime of reindeer.

Conclusion

A fascinating and significant species that lives in the Arctic and subarctic regions of North America, Europe, and Asia is the reindeer, also known as the caribou. They have unique physical and behavioral characteristics that allow them live in the extreme cold since they have been acclimated to the harsh conditions of their environment.

Several civilizations, especially those of Indigenous peoples and local communities, who depend on reindeer for subsistence, transportation, and cultural rituals, place a high value on reindeer. Being a keystone species that supports the vitality and diversity of Arctic and subarctic environments, they are also significant ecologically.

However, a number of concerns, including as habitat loss, climate change, predation, and overhunting, affect reindeer numbers. Reindeer populations are being preserved through the creation of protected areas, habitat restoration, limitations on hunting and poaching, and analysis of the effects of climate change and other dangers.

In general, reindeer population conservation is a continuing task that necessitates the cooperation and involvement of numerous diverse stakeholders. Together, we can make sure that these intriguing and significant animals survive and thrive in the wild for many years to come.

Thank you